Mark Grace

WINNING WITH GRACE

by
Barry Rozner

SPORTS PUBLISHING INC.
www.SportsPublishingInc.com

©1999 Sports Publishing Inc.
All rights reserved.

Production Manager: Susan M. McKinney
Cover design: Scot Muncaster
Photos: *The Associated Press*, Tustin High School, Tustin, CA,
and San Diego State University

ISBN: 1-58261-056-8
Library of Congress Catalog Card Number: 99-61948

SPORTS PUBLISHING INC.
sportspublishinginc.com

Printed in the United States.

CONTENTS

The "Hey Hey" patch on the Cubs jerseys in 1998 honored the late Jack Brickhouse. (AP/Wide World Photos)

Back to the Playoffs

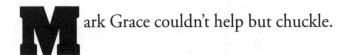

Mark Grace couldn't help but chuckle.

The Cubs were in the first wild-card tie-breaker in the history of baseball on September 28, 1998. The score was 5-3 in the top of the ninth, and the San Francisco Giants had the tying run at the plate in the form of 1993 World Series hero Joe Carter.

There were two outs, closer Rod Beck, already the owner of 50 thrilling saves, was on the mound and the Cubs were trying to make the playoffs for the first time since 1989.

There couldn't have been more drama even if it had been the seventh game of the World Series.

Even at the most harrowing moment of a season filled with so much stress and strife, Mark allowed his mind to wander for just a moment. While catcher Tyler Houston took a stroll out to the mound, Mark took a stroll down memory lane.

He looked over in the Giants' dugout and caught the eye of ex-Cubs shortstop Shawon Dunston, one of Mark's closest friends in the world. Dunston smiled and Mark started laughing.

"The thing is, when Shawon and I were young players, back in 1988 and 1989, both of us had a little trouble with the glove, if you know what I mean," Mark explained. "Shawon was throwing away about 30 balls a year and I was kicking about 20, or so it seemed.

"And whenever it would get to be near the end of a close game, Shawon and I would get nervous.

Then, I'd look to my right and Shawon would look to his left, and there would be Ryne Sandberg, the best fielding second baseman in the history of 130 years of baseball, standing right in between us.

"Shawon and I would be sweating and worried and there would Ryno, cool as can be, telling us where to play and what to expect. And Ryno was the type of guy who wanted the ball hit to him. I mean, he made four errors a year and when he made one, everyone figured he must have been sick or something, because it never happened. He won nine Gold Gloves in a row for a reason.

"And when he did make an error, it sure never happened late in a game, so Ryno was standing there hoping they'd hit it to him, and you know what, so were Shawon and I. That's why I was laughing that night at Wrigley Field with so much at stake.

"Because Shawon and I used to look across the field at each other, look at Ryno, and look back at

Mark, left, and former teammate Shawon Dunston, shown here sharing a laugh before a game in 1996, have come a long way since their days as young players who had "a little trouble with the glove." (AP/Wide World Photos)

each other and silently mouth the words, 'Hit it to Ryno.' That was our thing. 'Hit it to Ryno,' because when they did, you knew the game was over. He was our security blanket. That became our catch phrase.

"So that's why I was laughing when I saw Shawon in the Giants' dugout. We both knew what each other was thinking."

By 1998, Mark himself was a four-time Gold Glove winner and had come a long way since the days when he and Dunston were making errors by the bushel. Ryne Sandberg was gone, retired at the end of the 1997 season, and now Mark was standing there thinking, "Hit it to me."

That's exactly what happened.

Beck fooled Carter with an off-speed pitch and Carter popped it up. It was a soft but tricky, spinning fly that headed toward first base. There, 34-year-old Mark Grace, once a disaster in the field, but a man who had worked ferociously hard to improve himself, camped under the ball.

He put his glove up and his bare hand next to it just for safety and waited for what seemed like an eternity. Finally, the ball emerged from the lights, dropped softly and landed perfectly in the pocket of Mark's glove. He squeezed tight on the ball for the final out and Wrigley Field erupted in bedlam.

Mark became a statue.

"I kind of just stood there for a moment and thought, 'What an incredible year this has been. What an amazing journey we have witnessed.' I was just standing there thinking about it," he recalled. "And then I went nuts. I started running around jumping on guys and we wound up in a big pile in the middle of the field. It was such a relief and such exhilaration at the same time.

"It was the finish to an emotionally and physically exhausting season and I wanted that moment to last for a while. I didn't want to let go."

CHAPTER TWO

Team First

For Mark Grace, 1998 was simply another exceptional season. He hit over .300 for the eighth time in 11 years, bringing his career batting average to .310, and set a career high in homers with 17. He also drove in 89 runs, the eighth time he's posted RBI totals above 75. On top of that, he scored 92 runs, walked 93 times, collected 39 doubles and played a terrific first base.

Just another Mark Grace season.

"You didn't hear much about Mark in 1998 because so much else was happening with Sammy

Mark greets Cardinals slugger Mark McGwire as McGwire rounds the bases after hitting his record-breaking 62nd home run on September 8, 1998. (AP/Wide World Photos)

Sosa and Kerry Wood and everyone else," said Cubs manager Jim Riggleman. "But I'll tell you what, Mark Grace was great for us and we wouldn't have gotten where we did without him.

"It's not just that he plays so well, but he shows up every day and plays hard and he plays hurt. He batted almost 700 times when you include all those walks, and that means a lot. He's our leader, and you need your leader to show up and play hard and be there for his teammates, and that's what Mark Grace did for us."

Mark was much happier about what his team accomplished than what he or any of his teammates accomplished as individuals.

Yes, Sammy Sosa's MVP season and run for the home run record was incredible. Being in St. Louis to watch Mark McGwire hit home runs No. 61 and 62 was something he'll never forget. Kerry

Wood's 20-strikeout performance was amazing and his Rookie of the Year Award well-deserved.

But for Mark, it has always been about the team first and everything else second.

"I'll tell you what, I saw more things happen during the 1998 baseball season than I've ever seen happen in my life," Mark said. "It was probably the most exciting season I've ever been associated with, although winning the National League East in 1989 probably still takes the cake."

That's because Mark learned early on that playing the game correctly and winning games is what baseball is all about.

"You see, I broke into baseball with a different generation of players," Mark remembers. "That was back in the days when Don Zimmer was the manager and Rick Sutcliffe was the ace of the staff and we had three Hall of Famers on our team: Ryne Sandberg, Andre Dawson and Greg Maddux.

Mark as a junior at Tustin High School in Tustin, California. (Tustin High School)

"We had a lot of veterans who taught me how to play and the things we should do and shouldn't do, and the thing that was most important was the team."

Sutcliffe says Mark surprised the veterans with a toughness and team concept that belied his Southern California roots and long blond hair. He quickly warmed up to a crewcut and a Midwestern work ethic.

"He's one of those guys who really understands what it means to be a professional baseball player," Sutcliffe says. "That's hard to find these days. Gracie might be the last of a dying breed."

*Baseball wasn't the only sport Mark played in high school.
(Tustin High School)*

Mark says he owes it all to the impressive group of teammates he inherited.

"All of us had one thing in common: we wanted to win games," he said. "That's what it was all about and that's still the way I approach every game of every season, with the goal of getting to the World Series."

CHAPTER THREE

Growing Up

Long before he began dreaming of the World Series, Mark Eugene Grace was born in Winston-Salem, North Carolina, on June 28, 1964.

The family moved around quite a bit, but it didn't stop Mark from playing every sport imaginable. By the time he got to Tustin High School in southern California, his primary sporting interests were baseball and basketball, and it was becoming clear that he had a great future in one of the two games.

Mark's basketball team in his junior year at Tustin High School. Mark is far left in the top row. (Tustin High School)

Mark with his baseball team in his junior year in high school. (Tustin High School)

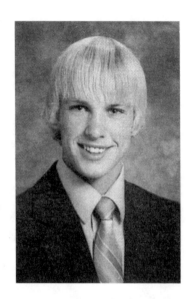

As a senior in high school, Mark was a member of the prom court (below, farthest to the left). (Tustin High School)

As a senior, Mark still played both basketball and baseball. Here he is shown with the basketball team. (Tustin High School)

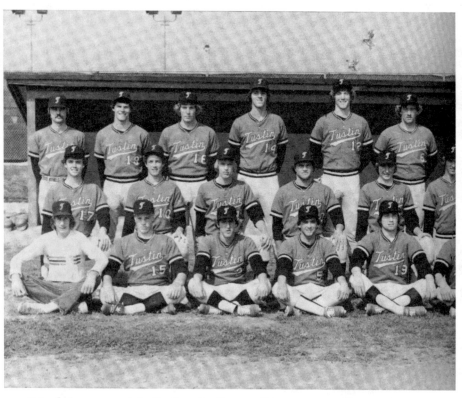

Mark (center, with the baseball team his senior year) says his parents taught him to always listen to his coaches. (Tustin High School)

Mark wasn't drafted by the Cubs until the 24th round of the 1985 draft. (San Diego State University)

Before being drafted by the Cubs, Mark played at San Diego State University. (San Diego State University)

He was always kept in line by his parents, Gene and Sharon, and Mark says that was the key to his development as a person and an athlete.

"When we moved to St. Louis, Keith Hernandez became my favorite baseball player, and when we moved to California, Magic Johnson became my favorite basketball player," Mark explains. "Those guys were my idols growing up, but my hero was—and still is—my father. He raised a family and put two kids through college, and to me, that's what being a hero really is.

"He and my mom are the best people I've ever known and they are the reason I made it in pro sports."

As a teenager, Mark learned to listen to his parents and believe in what they told him.

"My parents taught me a lot of great things, but maybe the most important thing in terms of sports was that they taught me to listen to my coaches," Mark says. "As a kid, you think you're so smart, but no matter how smart you think you are, your coaches know more than you do and the best thing you can do for your own development is listen to them. They know more than you do.

"Another thing my parents taught me was to stay away from drugs and gangs, because those things can kill you. I never forgot that."

Even with all of that advice and all of that talent, Mark's road to the big leagues wasn't an easy one. He graduated from Tustin High near Los Angeles in 1982 and attended Saddleback College in Mission Viejo, California, before transferring to San Diego State University, where he became a big-time baseball star.

Still, he hadn't convinced the major league scouts that he was a serious big league prospect. The Cubs waited until the 24th round to draft him in 1985, a far cry from the big bonuses and star treatment received by the first- and second-round picks.

He signed with the Cubs, and the following spring Mark, then 21, went to camp as a professional baseball player and made the most of his opportunity.

All he did in his first season as a pro in 1986 was hit .342 for Class A Peoria, Illinois, and win the Midwest League batting title, earning All-Star honors. He led the league in hits and drove home 95 runs.

Mark was on his way.

"The thing is, the Cubs gave me a chance," Mark said. "I'll always be grateful to (general manager) Dallas Green and the organization for drafting me and giving me a chance to play in the minors. And once I was there, they didn't look at me like a 24th-round guy. They gave me a fair shake and gave me a chance to make it if I performed well."

The following year, 1987, at Double A Pittsfield, Massachusetts, Mark was even better. He was selected the Eastern League's Most Valuable Player after hitting .333 with a league-high 101 RBI. He again made the All-Star team as he collected 54 extra-base hits and posted a .545 slugging percentage.

"That's as good of a season as I've ever seen a player have," says Mark's Pittsfield manager, Jim Essian. "You could see then that he was getting stronger and developing into a big league baseball player. There was no stopping him."

Now, this unknown, 24th-round draft choice wasn't so unknown anymore. In fact, there wasn't a question of whether Mark would make it to the majors, but rather, when would he make it to the majors?

Reaching the Big Leagues

After just two seasons in the minor leagues, Mark went to major league camp in the spring of 1988 and appeared to have little more than an outside shot at making the big league roster.

But he had a huge spring training, hitting everything that was thrown his way, and it looked like he was going to take the first base job away from veteran Leon Durham. He put new general manager Jim Frey and manager Don Zimmer in a tough position.

"They had a very popular player in Leon Durham and they had this kid setting the world on fire. It was a tough spot for them," Mark said. "They did what they had to do."

They gave Durham one more chance and sent Mark to Triple A Iowa to start the season. But on May 2, the inevitable occurred. Mark, then 23 years old, was called up and immediately put into the starting lineup while Durham went to the bench.

The first night, in front of all of his family and friends in San Diego, Mark collected two hits. The next night, he hit his first home run. The first month, he hit .330 and never looked back.

All the while, Leon Durham was sitting on the bench watching. On May 19, the Cubs traded Durham to Cincinnati and the Mark Grace era was officially underway in Chicago.

"Leon Durham was really a good dude," Mark says. "He was really good about it that spring when

I was playing well. He was very kind to me and very good to me. He really helped me. He said that Bill Buckner had done the same thing for him in a similar situation, and now he was returning the favor.

"I have a lot of respect for Leon Durham. He took it all in stride and treated me well. Not everyone would have done that, to be sure. He was kind to me even though he knew I was taking his job. He was very good about it and I'll always admire him for that."

Mark went on to hit .296 in his rookie campaign, earning him Rookie of the Year honors from *The Sporting News*. He finished sixth in the league in hitting and proved he belonged as a big leaguer.

"I was very fortunate to break into the league with a team like that, and I'll always be thankful to Jim Frey and Don Zimmer for giving me the chance to play in the big leagues," Mark said. "They called

Mark collides with Philadelphia Phillies catcher Mike Lieberthal while trying to score. The umpire called him out. (AP/Wide World Photos)

me up and once I got there, I said, 'I'm never going back.' And I never did."

Most importantly, Mark got to the big leagues as the era of enormous salaries was changing the game of baseball forever. Mark had the benefit of some excellent teaching, and never fell into the trap that so many young players do today.

"The guys on the team would never allow me to think about the money or the nightlife or all the distractions," Mark says. "They taught me how to be a baseball player and I consider myself lucky to have been around them."

Indeed, today Mark is considered a throwback to the days when players got their uniforms dirty and sacrificed their bodies for the team, something most superstars won't do anymore.

"When I got to the big leagues, I had the greatest examples of how to go about your job that you could ever have," Mark explained. "There was Ryne

Mark finishes rounding the bases after a home run.
(AP/Wide World Photos)

Sandberg and Andre Dawson in the locker room every day. They were the first ones in and the last ones to leave. They worked harder than anyone even though they were already superstars.

"They never took a day off, no matter how much they hurt, and they never skipped a day of batting practice or infield practice, no matter how tired they were. They were guys who taught you work ethic without ever having to say a word. They led by example, and you got the message. If the best players on the team, guys going to the Hall of Fame, never loafed, how could you?

"I remember during spring training, at 8 a.m. when most guys were just getting to the park and getting dressed, Ryno would already be out on the field taking an extra couple hundred groundballs before the workout even began. That's the kind of example I learned from.

"And these guys expected you to know how to play the game. Today, half the guys don't know what base to throw to or how to hit a cut-off man. When I broke in, there was none of that, because if you didn't know how to play, you weren't going to play because your teammates wouldn't put up with it.

"They forced you to respect the game, respect your teammates and respect yourself. Today, I'm afraid that players make so much money that their emphasis on those things is diminished. That never happened to me, but I had a lot of help along the way."

CHAPTER FIVE

Early Success

Now, if you think they don't have fun in the big leagues, think again.

In fact, just a few days after Mark made it up to the majors in 1988, veteran Rick Sutcliffe gave him a little tip.

"We were at Wrigley Field and there was a rain delay," Mark explains. "So I found Rick Sutcliffe and asked him where the indoor batting cages were, since I had never hit in them before. So Sut says, 'Go out this door here and walk all the way around to the right-field corner until you get to a big tent, and that's where the cages are.'

"Well, it turns out, Sut had sent me into the main concourse where all the fans are. I was in uniform so the fans were mobbing me, and it was a rain delay so the concourse was jammed. And here I am in my metal spikes, jogging through all these people with my bat in my hand, trying to find the batting cages. The first place I find happens to be the visitor's clubhouse, and there is Red Schoendienst, a coach for the Cardinals, looking at me like I'm crazy.

"Then, the next place I try is the big tent around the corner in right field, which happens to be a picnic area. So now, I realize Sut played a practical joke on me. I have to run back through the concourse again, all the way back to our clubhouse down the left-field line.

"I got back in and I said, 'OK, real funny. Now where are the cages?' Sut thought about it for a moment, and was prepared to send me to a local burger joint but he didn't have the heart. So finally, he told me how to get to the real cages underneath the right-field bleachers. But that was my introduction to Wrigley Field."

By 1989, Mark needed no introduction to Wrigley Field, and the fans of Chicago hardly needed to be introduced to Mark. After his regal rookie season, Mark followed it up with a spectacular sophomore season, helping lead the Cubs into the playoffs for only the second time since 1945.

"Some guys seem to go through that sophomore slump, but it didn't happen to Mark," remembers Ryne Sandberg. "He had a great year for us and we wouldn't have made the playoffs if he hadn't come up big. He really blossomed into a big-time player."

Mark not only hit .314 in his first full big-league season, but he also led the National League Eastern Division champs in RBI with 79.

Mark insists he was "just one of the guys" in 1989.
(AP/Wide World Photos)

"I was just one of the guys," he insists. "My gosh, we had Ryno hitting 30 homers; and Greg Maddux winning 19 games; and Mike Bielecki winning 18 games; and Mitch Williams scaring us to death every night and saving games; and Jerome Walton and Dwight Smith finishing 1-2 in Rookie of the Year voting.

"We had a lot of heroes. I was just one of the guys."

The week for which some people will always remember him occurred after the Cubs clinched the division. It was during the National League Championship Series against the San Francisco Giants that Mark took center stage and delivered the performance of his life.

Mark went 11-for-17 in five games against the Giants, batting an incredible .647 with three doubles, one triple, one home run, eight RBI and a 1.118 slugging percentage.

The problem is, the Cubs lost the series four games to one, and Mark's best chance to get to the World Series ended prematurely.

"It's still the thing people talk about when they see me. They want to talk about the series Will Clark and I had against each other," Mark said. "A lot of memorable things happened that year and during those playoffs and it's what got my career going. I was in the spotlight with Will Clark, and it kind of put the stamp on both of our careers.

"I learned a lot about winning and losing that year. I learned by watching the veterans on that team, and how they wanted to be there with the game on the line. I think Ryno hit about .400 the second half of the season and he pretty much carried us.

"And I watched guys like Ryno and Andre and Sut and Mad Dog handle the press after we lost to the Giants, the way they stood up and answered question after question, not hiding in the trainer's room.

"But the thing that bothers me about it is we didn't get to the World Series, because that was my best chance. All the games we lost were very close games and it was tough to swallow. Then, you see how hard it is to get back to the playoffs and you realize how young you were and what a great opportunity and experience it was.

"To me, it's all about winning, so the personal achievements of that postseason don't mean as much to me as they would have had we gotten to the big dance. Don't get me wrong, it was the greatest experience of my major league career because we won the division and we made the playoffs.

"But not getting to the World Series hurts, and I'll always remember that, too. There's always a little bitter with the sweet, you know, and the closer you come to the ultimate dream, the harder it is to accept defeat."

Hard Times in Chicago

Beginning in 1990, Mark found out how difficult it was to repeat as champs. The Cubs suffered a slew of injuries to the pitching staff, and they were pretty much out of the race by June.

Mark continued to improve as a player. He hit .309, good for sixth in the league, drove in a career-high 82 runs and began to make his mark defensively, setting the major league record for assists by a first baseman in a season with 180.

"I worked hard to become a good defensive player because it mattered to me. I wasn't born with it," Mark said. "But I had a lot of help, too."

Over the years, Mark has built a reputation as an outstanding defensive first baseman. (AP/Wide World Photos)

Mark has always been a good hitter, but has worked hard to become a better fielder. (AP/Wide World Photos)

Mark said many of his coaches were there for him when he needed extra groundballs and advice on how to play the position. Specifically, he says it was coach Joe Altobelli (1988-91) who spent tireless hours talking philosophy of fielding with him off the field, and on the field hitting him thousands of grounders.

"Mark was a very hard worker," Altobelli remembers. "He was a great hitter, everybody knew that. But he was very young when he came to the big leagues and I thought he could be a better fielder if he worked at it. He had great hands and great instinct. I felt like there was no reason he couldn't be a Gold Glove first baseman."

That didn't happen in 1991, but something bad did: Don Zimmer got fired. It was Mark's first experience seeing his manager get fired, and unfortunately for him and the Cubs, it was an experience he would have to get used to.

"We brought in three big free agents—George Bell, Danny Jackson and Dave Smith—before the 1991 season, and everyone thought that team, which was still pretty much together from 1989, was going to go to the World Series," Mark recalls. "But again, we had a bunch of injuries to the pitching staff and the worst thing was we just couldn't hold a lead late in the game. If Dave Smith was healthy, we would have had a first-rate closer and things would have looked much different.

"But we couldn't hold a lead and started to fall out of the race. Near the end of May, Zim got fired and it was pretty devastating. The players loved him and we felt responsible. If you don't feel responsible when your manager gets fired, you just don't get it."

Jim Essian was promoted to big league manager from Triple A, but his problem was the same as Zimmer's—injuries to the pitching staff made it impossible to compete. The Cubs fell out of the race, and Essian, a good friend of Mark's from their minor league days, also was fired at the end of the season.

"Two managers fired in four months. What a mess," Mark said. "It was a big mess and it took years to get it straightened out."

Mark felt the strain of losing games and losing managers in 1991 and saw his average slip seriously for the only time in his career. He dropped to .273 at the plate, but in the field the league was beginning to appreciate his potential. In 1992, he made just four errors and finally won his first Gold Glove.

He also rebounded at the plate with a strong season, batting .307, good for ninth in the league. The Cubs played well in 1992 under new manager Jim Lefebvre, and they pitched exceptionally well, but just didn't have enough offense to get it done. They were only a few games out of first with five

In 1993, Mark had career-high totals in hits (193) and RBI (98). (AP/Wide World Photos)

weeks to go, before the pitching staff and the season crumbled.

"The team was coming together under Jimmy and you could see the potential," Mark said. "All we had to do was keep our key players and we'd be OK."

But in the off-season, Greg Maddux was allowed to leave as a free agent, and that was the beginning of the end.

"We had a general manager (Larry Himes) who thought he was smarter than everyone else, and he thought we could get by without Greg Maddux," Mark said. "Here, the guy had just won 20 games and the Cy Young and we couldn't keep him on our team. That was the worst decision I've ever seen in baseball."

While Maddux went on to superstardom, the Cubs' pitching staff went to pieces. The Cubs hit the cover off the ball in 1993, led by Mark, who

Mark says Jim LeFebvre, who managed the Cubs in 1992 and 1993, was the best hitting coach he's ever had. (AP/Wide World Photos)

had the biggest offensive output of his career up to that point. He batted .325 (fifth in the league) and had career highs in hits (193) and RBI (98), to go along with 39 doubles and 14 homers.

He also won his second straight Gold Glove.

"I think Mark Grace is one of the best pure hitters I've ever seen," says Lefebvre. "And I managed Ken Griffey Jr. and I was a hitting coach for Mark McGwire.

"Mark will never be a big power guy, but that doesn't really matter, because he drives in runs and hits a lot of doubles. Hey, I'll take a guy who can hit .320 and be a team leader and play great defense any time. Besides, if he can stay healthy and play six or seven more years at the same level, people are going to start talking about him as one of the best hitters ever."

That's high praise coming from Lefebvre, but he and Mark always had a special bond. Unfortunately, their time together was short. Despite the team's strong second half in 1993 and their furious effort to save the manager's job, another one bit the dust.

"That was a just a case of our manager being a popular guy and the general manager wasn't popular, so he fired the manager," Mark said. "That was crushing for the team, because we loved Jimmy and we played hard for him. In 1993, the Phillies jumped out to about a 20-game lead on everyone and we had no chance. Plus, our pitching staff was a mess without Maddux and we had some tough injuries again.

"But we played great the second half and posted a winning record and thought we had saved Jimmy's job. We were wrong. It was a bad time. Jim Lefebvre was the best hitting coach I've ever had and I was very sorry to see him go."

It was more of the same the next year as the emotionally bankrupt club failed to deliver for new manager Tom Trebelhorn, another good guy who deserved a better fate. The Cubs were so bad that by the time the strike occurred in mid-August, everyone was ready to head home.

Again, Mark felt the strain of an awful situation. He hit only .298 with 44 RBI, and watched former teammate after former teammate succeed against his team. Ex-Cubs Danny Jackson, Rick Sutcliffe, Bob Tewksbury, Shawn Boskie and Greg Maddux were just a few of the pitchers who stuck it to the Cubs in 1994.

"It was a disaster," Mark said. "I was starting to think I might have to leave Chicago if I ever wanted to play for a winner, and that was something I didn't want to do."

Things are Looking Up

Mark was scheduled to be a free agent after the 1994 season, but with no conclusion to the labor strife, months and months went by and he had no team.

In the meantime, the Cubs' front office underwent a big change. The old regime was dismissed and in came a new group and a fresh attitude. When the strike finally ended, Mark had to make a choice between the Cubs and the south side White Sox, who were seriously courting him.

Mark celebrates a game-winning hit. (AP/Wide World Photos)

Mark, left, Sammy Sosa, center, Scott Servais, right, and Manny Alexander celebrate after a victory at home in Wrigley Field. (AP/Wide World Photos)

"I had guys like Frank Thomas and Robin Ventura calling me up and trying to convince me to come play first base for the White Sox," Mark said. "The new management with (team president) Andy MacPhail didn't know me and I didn't know them. I was concerned about having a chance to win. I decided I'd give it one more year and see what happened.

"And what a year it was."

A new feeling had come over the north side of Chicago under new manager Jim Riggleman and Mark responded with perhaps the best year of his career. He hit .326 with a league-leading 51 doubles, a career-high 16 homers and 92 RBI, while picking up his third Gold Glove in four years.

Mark also found out what it was like to be in contention again, as the first year of the wild card race proved to be an advantage for the Cubs. Long gone from the new Central Division race, Mark and

Mark tosses a bat to fans in the bleachers during a rain delay at Wrigley Field. (AP/Wide World Photos)

the Cubs hung in the wild card battle until the final 48 hours of the season.

They posted thrilling comeback win after thrilling comeback win, and the new energy brought out Mark's best. He hit .516 the final week of the season with nine runs scored and nine RBI in seven games as he captured Player of the Week honors.

"It was fun to be back in the thick of it again for the first time since 1989," Mark said. "I was beginning to think I might never feel that excitement again."

After another All-Star season, Mark was now a free agent again, but having proved himself yet again to yet another new management team, the Cubs fought off challenges from Mark's boyhood favorites, the Cardinals, and re-signed Mark to a long-term deal.

"It was touch and go, and I was prepared to go," Mark says with a chuckle. "But the Cubs came

Mark began the 1999 season with 1,875 hits. (AP/Wide World Photos)

up with the right offer at the right time and I was glad, because I would hate to ever leave the Cubs."

Mark came back with a career-high .331 in 1996 and collected his fourth Gold Glove, while the Cubs stayed in the race until the final 10 days of the season. But 1997 was another disaster as the Cubs dropped their first 14 games of the season. That didn't stop Mark from batting .319 and driving in 88 runs.

Then, came the miracle season of 1998, which will leave Cubs fans with a taste of what can happen when all the stars align properly. Getting swept by the Braves in the playoffs was also a reminder that making the playoffs is a far cry from winning the World Series, which remains Mark's ultimate goal.

Mark began the 1999 season with 1,875 hits, and if he continues to average 180 a season, which he does in most non-strike years, Grace could reach

Coach Dan Radison, right, hugs Mark after Mark's game-winning single in 1996. (AP/Wide World Photos)

3,000 hits in a little more than six years, or shortly after the start of the 2005 season.

"If I stay healthy and keep playing well, that's a possibility," Mark concedes. "That's a goal of mine. If I have any type of year this season, I'll pass 2,000 hits, and then I can start thinking about 3,000. That would be very special to me because 3,000 is pretty much automatic Hall of Fame, like 500 homers.

"That's a long way away, if it ever happens. Right now, all I think about is getting into the World Series. I look at all the guys I played with like Ryne Sandberg and Andre Dawson, who never got to play in a World Series, and I know how bad they felt about that.

"I know that they wanted it for themselves and for Cubs fans, who deserve it more than any fans in the world. Gosh, if I could get to a World Series..."

Mark didn't bother to finish the sentence. He didn't have to.

Mark Grace Quick Facts

Full Name: Mark Eugene Grace
Team: Chicago Cubs
Hometown: Winston-Salem, North Carolina
Position: First Baseman
Jersey Number: 17
Bats: Left
Throws: Left
Height: 6-2
Weight: 195 pounds
Birthdate: June 28, 1964

1998 Highlight: Helped lead the Cubs to the National League playoffs.

Stats Spotlight: Hit a career-high 17 home runs in 1998.

Little-Known Fact: During the decade of the 1990s, only Tony Gwynn (1,574) has more hits than Mark Grace (1,571).

Mark singles in two runs against the Pirates. (AP/Wide World Photos)

Mark and Coach Dan Radison celebrate a Cubs victory.
(AP/Wide World Photos)

Mark Grace's Professional Career

Year	Club	AVG	G	AB	R	H	2B	3B	HR	RBI	BB	SO	SB
1986	Peoria-A	.342*	126	465	81	159+	30	4	15	95	60	28	6
1987	Pittsfield-AA	.333	123	453	81	151	29	8	17	101*	48	24	5
1988	Iowa-AAA	.254	21	67	11	17	4	0	0	14	13	4	1
	Cubs	.296	134	486	65	144	23	4	7	57	60	43	3
1989	Cubs	.314	142	510	74	160	28	3	13	79	80	42	14
1990	Cubs	.309	157	589	72	182	32	1	9	82	59	54	15
1991	Cubs	.273	160	619*	87	169	28	5	8	58	70	53	3
1992	Cubs	.307	158	603	72	185	37	5	9	79	72	36	6
1993	Cubs	.325	155	594	86	193	39	4	14	98	71	32	8
1994	Cubs	.298	106	403	55	120	23	3	6	44	48	41	0
1995	Cubs	.326	143	552	97	180	51*	3	16	92	65	46	6
1996	Cubs	.331	142	547	88	181	39	1	9	75	62	41	2
1997	Cubs	.319	151	555	87	177	32	5	13	78	88	45	2
1998	Cubs	.309	158	595	92	184	39	3	17	89	93	56	4

M.L./Cubs Totals   .310 1606 6053 875 1875 371 37 121 831 768 489 63

*Led League   +Tied for League Lead

	Pinch-Hitting						Fielding			
AVG	AB	H	HR	RBI		PCT	PO	A	E	TC
.500	2	1	0	2	1998	.994	1279	122	8	1409
.313	32	10	0	7	Career	.995	14168	1354	84	15606

All-Star Game

Year	Club/Site	AVG	G	AB	R	H	2B	3B	HR	RBI	BB	SO	SB
1993	N.L./Bal	.000	1	3	0	0	0	0	0	0	0	0	0
1995	N.L./Tex	.000	1	0	0	0	0	0	0	0	0	0	0
1997	N.L./Cle	.000	1	1	0	0	0	0	0	0	0	0	0
Totals		**.000**	**3**	**4**	**0**	**0**	**0**	**0**	**0**	**0**	**0**	**0**	**0**

Divisional Series

Year	Club	AVG	G	AB	R	H	2B	3B	HR	RBI	BB	SO	SB
1998	CUBS v. Atl	.083	3	12	0	1	0	0	0	1	0	2	0

League Championship Series

Year	Club	AVG	G	AB	R	H	2B	3B	HR	RBI	BB	SO	SB
1989	CUBS v. SF	.647	5	17	3	11	3	1	1	8	4	1	1

Mark congratulates Sammy Sosa on another home run.
(AP/Wide World Photos)

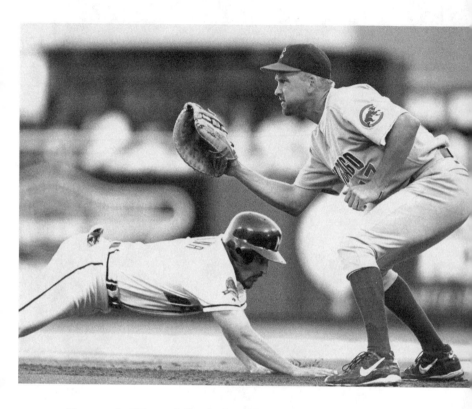

Fernando Vina of the Milwaukee Brewers slides safely back to first under Mark's watchful eye. (AP/Wide World Photos)

1990s Hits Leaders

Tony Gwynn	1574
Mark Grace	**1571**
Paul Molitor	1568
Rafael Palmeiro	1564
Craig Biggio	1540

1990s Singles Leaders

Tony Gwynn	1160
Mark Grace	**1120**
Paul Molitor	1104
Lance Johnson	1090
Craig Biggio	1079

Mark is one of three Cubs to win Gold Glove awards in the 1990s. (AP/Wide World Photos)

1990s Doubles Leaders

Edgar Martinez	323
Mark Grace	**320**
Rafael Palmeiro	313
Albert Belle	308
Craig Biggio	306

Cubs Gold Glove Winners in the 1990s

Winner	Year	Position
Mark Grace	1996	1B
Mark Grace	1995	1B
Mark Grace	1993	1B
Mark Grace	1992	1B
Greg Maddux	1992	P
Ryne Sandberg	1991	2B
Greg Maddux	1991	P
Ryne Sandberg	1990	2B
Greg Maddux	1990	P

One of the highlights of Mark's career was watching Sammy Sosa's incredible 1998 season. (AP/Wide World Photos)

Mark Grace's Major League Career Fielding Statistics

Year	PCT	G	PO	A	E	TC	DP
1988	.987	133	1182	87	17	1286	91
1989	.996	142	1230	126	6	1362	93
1990	.992	153	1324	180+*#	12	1516	116
1991	.995	160#	1520#	167#	8	1695#	106
1992^	.998*	157	1580#	141*	4	1725#	119
1993^	.997	154	1456#	112	5	1573#	134#
1994	.993	103	925	78	7	1010	91
1995^	.995	143	1211	114	7	1332	93
1996^	.997	141	1259	107	4	1370	120
1997	.995	148	1202	120	6	1328	93
1998	.994	156	1279	122	8	1409	82
Totals	.995*	1590*	14168*	1354*	84	15606*	1138

^Gold Glove Award Winner

#Major League Leader

+National League Record

*National League Leader

*Cubs Record

Top 10 Batting Average Finishes

Year	AVG	N.L. Rank
1988	.296	6th
1989	.314	4th
1990	.309	6th (tie)
1992	.307	9th
1993	.325	5th
1995	.326	5th
1996	.331	5th
1997	.319	6th

Career Transactions

Selected by Minnesota in 15th round of 1984 January draft—did not sign

Selected by Cubs in 24th round of 1985 June draft (Scout: Spider Jorgensen)

Chicago Cubs
Career Batting Average Leaders
(Average as Cubs player)

Riggs Stephenson	.336
Bill Madlock	.336
Bill Lange	.330
Cap Anson	.329
Kiki Cuyler	.325
Bill Everitt	.323
Hack Wilson	.322
Mike Kelly	.316
George Gore	.315
Mark Grace	**.310**

Chicago Cubs
Career Hits Leaders
(Hits as Cubs player)

Cap Anson	2,995
Ernie Banks	2,583
Billy Williams	2,510
Ryne Sandberg	2,385
Stan Hack	2,193
Ron Santo	2,171
Jimmy Ryan	2,073
Phil Cavarretta	1,927
Mark Grace	**1,875**
Gabby Hartnett	1,867

Chicago Cubs
Career Doubles Leaders
(Doubles as Cubs player)

Cap Anson	528
Ernie Banks	407
Ryne Sandberg	403
Billy Williams	402
Gabby Hartnett	391
Mark Grace	**371**
Stan Hack	363
Jimmy Ryan	362
Ron Santo	353
Billy Herman	346

Chicago Cubs
Career RBI Leaders
(RBI as Cubs player)

Cap Anson	1,879
Ernie Banks	1,636
Billy Williams	1,453
Ron Santo	1,290
Gabby Hartnett	1,153
Ryne Sandberg	1,061
Jimmy Ryan	914
Phil Cavarretta	896
Bill Nicholson	833
Mark Grace	**831**

Chicago Cubs
Hits Leaders by Decade
(Hits as Cubs player)

1900-09	Frank Chance	1,062
1910-19	Heinie Zimmerman	1,027
1920-29	Sparky Adams	780
1930-39	Billy Herman	1,540
1940-49	Phil Cavarretta	1,304
1950-59	Ernie Banks	1,051
1960-69	Billy Williams	1,651
1970-79	Don Kessinger	937
1980-89	Ryne Sandberg	1,394
1990-98	**Mark Grace**	**1,571**

Mark is the Cubs' team leader in hits in the 1990s.
(AP/Wide World Photos)

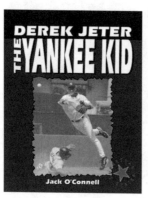

Derek Jeter:
The Yankee Kid

Author: Jack O'Connell
ISBN: 1-58261-043-6

In 1996 Derek burst onto the scene as one of the most promising young shortstops to hit the big leagues in a long time. His hitting prowess and ability to turn the double play have definitely fulfilled the early predictions of greatness.

A native of Kalamazoo, MI, Jeter has remained well grounded. He patiently signs autographs and takes time to talk to the young fans who will be eager to read more about him in this book.

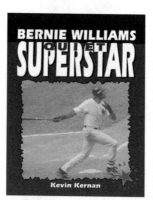

Bernie Williams:
Quiet Superstar

Author: Kevin Kernan
ISBN: 1-58261-044-4

Bernie Williams, a guitar-strumming native of Puerto Rico, is not only popular with his teammates, but is considered by top team officials to be the heir to DiMaggio and Mantle fame.

He draws frequent comparisons to Roberto Clemente, perhaps the greatest player ever from Puerto Rico. Like Clemente, Williams is humble, unassuming, and carries himself with quiet dignity. Also like Clemente, he plays with rare determination and a special elegance. He's married, and serves as a role model not only for his three children, but for his young fans here and in Puerto Rico.

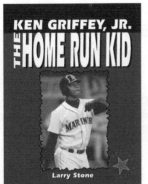

Larry Stone

Ken Griffey, Jr.:
The Home Run Kid

Author: Larry Stone
ISBN: 1-58261-041-x

Capable of hitting majestic home runs, making breathtaking catches, and speeding around the bases to beat the tag by a split second, Ken Griffey, Jr. is baseball's Michael Jordan. Amazingly, Ken reached the Major Leagues at age 19, made his first All-Star team at 20, and produced his first 100 RBI season at 21.

The son of Ken Griffey, Sr., Ken is part of the only father-son combination to play in the same outfield together in the same game, and, like Barry Bonds, he's a famous son who turned out to be a better player than his father.

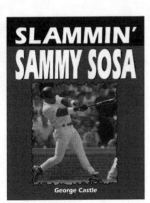

George Castle

Sammy Sosa:
Slammin' Sammy

Author: George Castle
ISBN: 1-58261-029-0

1998 was a break-out year for Sammy as he amassed 66 home runs, led the Chicago Cubs into the playoffs and finished the year with baseball's ultimate individual honor, MVP.

When the national spotlight was shone on Sammy during his home run chase with Mark McGwire, America got to see what a special person he is. His infectious good humor and kind heart have made him a role model across the country.

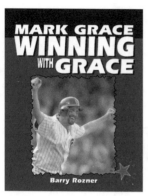

Mark Grace: Winning with Grace

Author: Barry Rozner
ISBN: 1-58261-056-8

This southern California native and San Diego State alumnus has been playing baseball in the windy city for nearly fifteen years. Apparently the cold hasn't affected his game. Mark is an all-around player who can hit to all fields and play great defense.

Mark's outgoing personality has allowed him to evolve into one of Chicago's favorite sons. He is also community minded and some of his favorite charities include the Leukemia Society of America and Easter Seals.

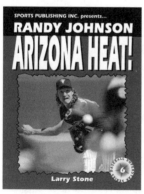

Randy Johnson: Arizona Heat!

Author: Larry Stone
ISBN: 1-58261-042-8

One of the hardest throwing pitchers in the Major Leagues, and, at 6'10" the tallest, the towering figure of Randy Johnson on the mound is an imposing sight which strikes fear into the hearts of even the most determined opposing batters.

Perhaps the most amazing thing about Randy is his consistency in recording strikeouts. He is one of only four pitchers to lead the league in strikeouts for four consecutive seasons. With his recent signing with the Diamondbacks, his career has been rejuvenated and he shows no signs of slowing down.

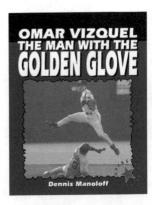

Omar Vizquel:
The Man with the Golden Glove
Author: Dennis Manoloff
ISBN: 1-58261-045-2

Omar has a career fielding percentage of .982 which is the highest career fielding percentage for any shortstop with at least 1,000 games played.

Omar is a long way from his hometown of Caracas, Venezuela, but his talents as a shortstop put him at an even greater distance from his peers while he is on the field.

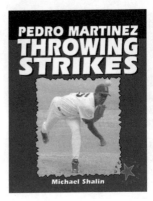

Pedro Martinez:
Throwing Strikes
Author: Mike Shalin
ISBN: 1-58261-047-9

The 1997 National League Cy Young Award winner is always teased because of his boyish looks. He's sometimes mistaken for the batboy, but his curve ball and slider leave little doubt that he's one of the premier pitchers in the American League.

It is fitting that Martinez is pitching in Boston, where the passion for baseball runs as high as it does in his native Dominican Republic.

Nomar Garciaparra: High 5!

Author: Mike Shalin
ISBN: 1-58261-053-3

An All-American at Georgia Tech, a star on the 1992 U.S. Olympic Team, the twelfth overall pick in the 1994 draft, and the 1997 American League Rookie of the Year, Garciaparra has exemplified excellence on every level.

At shortstop, he'll glide deep into the hole, stab a sharply hit grounder, then throw out an opponent on the run. At the plate, he'll uncoil his body and deliver a clutch double or game-winning homer. Nomar is one of the game's most complete players.

Juan Gonzalez: Juan Gone!

Author: Evan Grant
ISBN: 1-58261-048-7

One of the most prodigious and feared sluggers in the major leagues, Gonzalez was a two-time home run king by the time he was 24 years old.

After having something of a personal crisis in 1996, the Puerto Rican redirected his priorities and now says baseball is the third most important thing in his life after God and family.

SUPERSTAR SERIES

Mo Vaughn:
Angel on a Mission
Author: Mike Shalin
ISBN: 1-58261-046-0

Growing up in Connecticut, this Angels slugger learned the difference between right and wrong and the value of honesty and integrity from his parents early on, lessons that have stayed with him his whole life.

This former American League MVP was so active in Boston charities and youth programs that he quickly became one of the most popular players ever to don the Red Sox uniform.

Mo will be a welcome addition to the Angels line-up and the Anaheim community.

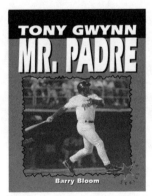

Tony Gwynn:
Mr. Padre
Author: Barry Bloom
ISBN: 1-58261-049-5

Tony is regarded as one of the greatest hitters of all-time. He is one of only three hitters in baseball history to win eight batting titles (the others: Ty Cobb and Honus Wagner).

In 1995 he won the Branch Rickey Award for Community Service by a major leaguer. He is unfailingly humble and always accessible, and he holds the game in deep respect. A throwback to an earlier era, Gwynn makes hitting look effortless, but no one works harder at his craft.

Kevin Brown:
That's Kevin with a "K"
Author: Jacqueline Salman
ISBN: 1-58261-050-9

Kevin was born in McIntyre, Georgia and played college baseball for Georgia Tech. Since then he has become one of baseball's most dominant pitchers and when on top of his game, he is virtually unhittable.

Kevin transformed the Florida Marlins and San Diego Padres into World Series contenders in consecutive seasons, and now he takes his winning attitude and talent to the Los Angeles Dodgers.

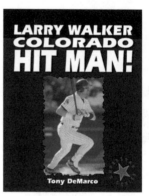

Larry Walker:
Colorado Hit Man!
Author: Tony DeMarco
ISBN: 1-58261-052-5

Growing up in Canada, Larry had his sights set on being a hockey player. He was a skater, not a slugger, but when a junior league hockey coach left him off the team in favor of his nephew, it was hockey's loss and baseball's gain.

Although the Rockies' star is known mostly for his hitting, he has won three Gold Glove awards, and has worked hard to turn himself into a complete, all-around ballplayer. Larry became the first Canadian to win the MVP award.

Sandy and Roberto Alomar:
Baseball Brothers

Author: Barry Bloom
ISBN: 1-58261-054-1

Sandy and Roberto Alomar are not just famous baseball brothers they are also famous baseball sons. Sandy Alomar, Sr. played in the major leagues fourteen seasons and later went into management. His two baseball sons have made names for themselves and have appeared in multiple All-Star games.

With Roberto joining Sandy in Cleveland, the Indians look to be a front-running contender in the American League Central.

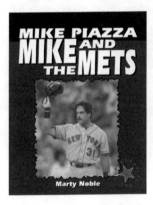

Mike Piazza:
Mike and the Mets

Author: Marty Noble
ISBN: 1-58261-051-7

A total of 1,389 players were selected ahead of Mike Piazza in the 1988 draft, who wasn't picked until the 62nd round, and then only because Tommy Lasorda urged the Dodgers to take him as a favor to his friend Vince Piazza, Mike's father.

Named in the same breath with great catchers of another era like Bench, Dickey and Berra, Mike has proved the validity of his father's constant reminder "If you work hard, dreams do come true."

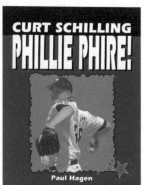

Curt Schilling: Phillie Phire!

Author: Paul Hagen
ISBN: 1-58261-055-x

Born in Anchorage, Alaska, Schilling has found a warm reception from the Philadelphia Phillies faithful. He has amassed 300+ strikeouts in the past two seasons and even holds the National League record for most strikeouts by a right handed pitcher at 319.

This book tells of the difficulties Curt faced being traded several times as a young player, and how he has been able to deal with off-the-field problems.

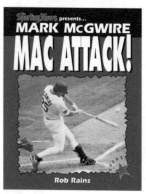

Mark McGwire: Mac Attack!

Author: Rob Rains
ISBN: 1-58261-004-5

Mac Attack! describes how McGwire overcame poor eyesight and various injuries to become one of the most revered hitters in baseball today. He quickly has become a legendary figure in St. Louis, the home to baseball legends such as Stan Musial, Lou Brock, Bob Gibson, Red Schoendienst and Ozzie Smith. McGwire thought about being a police officer growing up, but he hit a home run in his first Little League at-bat and the rest is history.

Roger Clemens: Rocket Man!

Author: Kevin Kernan
ISBN: 1-58261-128-9

Alex Rodriguez: A-plus Shortstop

ISBN: 1-58261-104-1

Baseball
SuperStar Series Titles

Collect Them All!

____ Sandy and Roberto Alomar: Baseball Brothers

____ Kevin Brown: Kevin with a "K"

____ Roger Clemens: Rocket Man!

____ Juan Gonzalez: Juan Gone!

____ Mark Grace: Winning With Grace

____ Ken Griffey, Jr.: The Home Run Kid

____ Tony Gwynn: Mr. Padre

____ Derek Jeter: The Yankee Kid

____ Randy Johnson: Arizona Heat!

____ Pedro Martinez: Throwing Strikes

____ Mike Piazza: Mike and the Mets

____ Alex Rodriguez: A-plus Shortstop

____ Curt Schilling: Philly Phire!

____ Sammy Sosa: Slammin' Sammy

____ Mo Vaughn: Angel on a Mission

____ Omar Vizquel: The Man with a Golden Glove

____ Larry Walker: Colorado Hit Man!

____ Bernie Williams: Quiet Superstar

____ Mark McGwire: Mac Attack!

Available by calling 877-424-BOOK